The

POSSIBLE PAST

AISLINN HUNTER

POLESTAR

An Imprint of Raincoast Books

Raincoast and Polestar acknowledge the ongoing financial support of the Government of Canada through The Canada Council for the Arts and the Book Publishing Industry Development Program (BPIDP); and the Government of British Columbia through the BC Arts Council.

Editor: Lynn Henry
Cover design: Val Speidel

National Library of Canada Cataloguing in Publication

Hunter, Aislinn, 1969–
    Possible past / Aislinn Hunter.

    ISBN 1-55192-721-7

    I. Title.

PS8565.U5766P67 2004   C811'.6   C2004-901962-7

Library of Congress Control Number: 2004092404

In the United States:
Publishers Group West
1700 Fourth Street
Berkeley, California
USA 94710

Polestar Book Publishers/Raincoast Books
9050 Shaughnessy Street
Vancouver, British Columbia
Canada, V6P 6E5
www.raincoast.com

At Raincoast Books we are committed to protecting the environment and to the responsible use of natural resources. We are acting on this commitment by working with suppliers and printers to phase out our use of paper produced from ancient forests. This book is one step towards that goal. It is printed on 100% ancient-forest-free paper (40% post-consumer recycled), processed chlorine- and acid-free, and supplied by New Leaf paper. It is printed with vegetable-based inks. For further information, visit our website at www.raincoast.com. We are working with Markets Initiative (www.oldgrowthfree.com) on this project.

Printed in Canada by Houghton Boston.
10 9 8 7 6 5 4 3 2 1

For Glenn

Contents

All writing is a species of remembering.

— Susan Sontag

"What can be conceived, is possible."

— Ludwig Wittgenstein

I.

ERRORS, INVENTIONS

Attempts to Know the Past

I do not want to say *darkness* or *door*,
or *the dark door we walk in through*.
This is no way to understand the past.
Will write instead of those regions on maps
coloured in by the imagination. Or the dusk
that is the backdrop of the universe —
how, when I was a child, I pictured space
hanging like a painting on a huge white canvas
inside a gilded frame. Infinity a notion that could
send a person over the edge, as in those Sinbad films
where whole ships careen over earth's steep curb,
and men gallop past the known periphery,
flogging their animals into the sea.

I will not write of the absence of light,
God's holy show, ripe orchards tilting their fruit
to the heavens. Or of the sun tossed like a gold coin
into the bucket of the sky. Instead I'll praise
what I have before me: a book, a lamp,
a chair beside the open window, a pocket watch
whose hour is caught in the glass eye of the moon.
The thread of history as dun-coloured
as a corridor in a painting by Vermeer.
Knock once on a street in Delf, watch a woman
asleep at her table, look through the slant

entrance to the room beyond. All these portals,
apertures that could take us anywhere.

The womb a door. The past a door. There,
I've said it. The future a bright yellow bird
in the corner of the room, singing. How easily
we fall off the map, sail into new worlds distracted
by song. Once, I stood in the National Museum lost
for hours in the radiant sheen of a pearl earring.
Terrible monsters here, they said, of those realms
where anything could happen, where anything
did happen. Who was I yesterday? The day before?
How have the rooms of the past remembered me,
if they remember me at all? Open a door onto the pitch
of space, onto the sunless caves we came from.
What sadness there, what hope, what delirium.

The Greeks March into the
Land of the Taochians

The Greeks were retreating to the sea.
There was no need for bloodshed.
Men stopping in six feet of snow saw the world
vanish around them — and stood there — dying
from cold or hunger. The black ends of their bodies
breaking open like strange flowers. And always
the enemy behind them, following the sandal trail
of dropt men, drifts dotted with the dark hides of oxen.
And so I would question what some call victory.
Is it the simple act of carrying on, or something greater?
And this poem will not make it beautiful: the towns
the Greeks took for livestock, the Taochians
who threw themselves from cliffs to avoid capture,
who followed their children to the ground.
A flight of terror, shock of the end and nothing
transcendent about it. No honour, no faith, no conquest,
only this — choosing the last thing one sees.
The town picked clean, the Greeks trudged on,
numb in their skirts of snow, a hundred baying
sheep roped behind them.
On the fifth day they reached the mountain;
other accounts would have them reach the sea.
But here, clouds gather across Theches
and they stagger awhile, lost in the darkness;
holding on to a cliff-edge, and the mercy
of gods they cannot see.

Variation on the Pietà

Let's say everyone's attention had shifted
to the thief on Christ's right. Maybe he had
the kind of brown eyes whole cultures fall into,
maybe he'd started to cry. And while
Christ was trying to summon the exact words
for what he needed to say, everyone turned
because the thief mumbled *Why?*
His mother at his feet beating his legs with her fists.
Maybe disappointment is that universal —
the crowd swaying in their sandals to see a man
berated for what he might have become, for failed
expectations. Then, his sheepish shrug, the one that is in
all of us, the desire to give up and take what comes.
What would have been ushered through the ages then?
The story of a man who had eight children
and not enough to feed them. The parable of the fat
goat tied to the post in the neighbour's yard.
The gospel that tells us how the thief crawled over
a stone wall with a knife in his teeth, how he severed the rope
and threw the animal over his shoulder while it bleated.
Found out in the searchlight of the moon. A man
who would do it all again, but who would slit
the animal's throat to avoid capture.

Imagine the commandments we'd have written
in the old books then: bind the mouth, slice open
the stomach, reach in with your hand, find the artery
between heart and brain, pinch it.
Wait until the animal dies, then untie it from its post
and carry it home in your arms like a child.

Hedge

Memory, a post you walk around:
The garden shears, the hedge, the peel of light cutting through.
A Sunday. Everyone proper was at church.
He stood on the far side of the hawthorn gutting a hole
through its centre. You wore a green summer dress,
your mother's pearls stolen from the top drawer of her dresser.
The clouds raced in from the sea, then sat sifting the sun.
You told him to stop it, said he was ruining the hedge.
Once, you found a rag tied to its highest branch — a wish
made on the road to town. Once, you tied a ribbon there yourself.
It became the property of a crow.
The shears made a clacking sound. Steady as a horse on the road.
Even the dog went back to the house after an hour of barking.
The grass that was kneeling east, kneeled west.
Birds swallowed their notes of protest.
Look: a boy on the cusp of being a man making his way to you
through a brown wheel of branches. His breath raspy as he drops
the shears, comes over, leads you to the gully and pins you down.
Look: the wagging fingers of cattails. The hole in the hawthorn
carrying the sky like a mirror.
How happy he is — a man who believes he's made something
from nothing. A wreath of twigs in his hair.
Later he will dream up houses that never materialize,
he will invent plans and means of escape. Your marriage
will become a search for exits.
But the sky, at present, is seamless and bright.

Even the hole in the hedge has its symmetry. And you
are a romantic, believe he has shown you his wounds,
steered a course through dark woods to find you.
After a while the crows come, ferrying the sound of church bells.
He gets up off you, pulls you from the dirt.
Then he turns into a pebble and you slip him into your pocket.
Now there are days when you take him out, measure
the heft of him in your hand.
Smooth on one side, flawed on the other. A stone to skip
across the river, to reel into the dark hole of the sea.
Look: the dark hole of the sea.
The bird on the post could be anyone.

Shadow Life

The afternoon gathers itself and folds into an envelope of evening.
The *what ifs* begin at the door.

A house as familiar as the Brahms I learned as a child —
every note, the whole arrangement.

The minute hand, the hour. The grandfather clock
minding itself on the wall.

Here, chairs that already have my shape in them.
Books I've read on the shelves.

Not a *what if*, but a question of *inhabitance*. My dresses filling her closet;
her sorrows close to, but not exactly, mine.

Upstairs, a strand of my hair on her pillow. In the garden, foxglove
I would have planted, were it not already there.

The mirror in the dining room casting candlelight
onto a landscape of plates and glasses.

Bone china, polished silver. Whole afternoons remembered,
staring out a window not my own.

Later he'll pass me a glass of wine and I'll know exactly
the span of his hands.

      What night did I sit up in the bed of this other life,
            push back
      the covers and walk away from the body beside me?

And what misstep has brought me here?

Somewhere there's a corner that turns into the possibility
of this existence.

The woman beside me having walked past it herself,
and lost something she went back to reclaim.

In this Spinning World, Who Knows Which is Up?

In every second Gallery in this Museum
    A student with an easel

Paintings copied in three-quarter scale —
    The tilted world, its plates of pears,

Boar hunts, ruined cities,
    Made smaller and still.

Here, a wedding portrait cast back into the dim
    Clockwork of a convex mirror.

Elsewhere, terrible celebrations, staged grief
    The held expression of duty.

Saint Sebastian tethered in a dark wood
    Where owls once purled

Through a painter's imagination.
    A deathbed curtain lightly drawn.

    All this stillness.

Outside: Paris. Bells that enter the hour,
    A schoolyard of boys in blue sweaters.

Consider, here, the history
of the tableau:

How there was a time when mirrors were hung
Too high to cast back our reflections.

How all we could see was the room
Of the childhood we stood in.

It isn't the gods we are trying to please,
all this re-creation.

The frayed border of tapestry
Dropped as fettle to the floor

Cannot be resewn.

And what did it contain?
A boy no historian could name

Two splay-legged mongrels,
Thread in russet.

What sets one canvas apart from another
Is surprise.

The Virgin in the one painting
    Who does not know what the angel will say.

Yes, it's true,
    A man once took my face in his hands,

Tilted the shallow pool of it
    Up

            And did not kiss me.

And it's said that in art the arrows
    Do not quiver.

In a Village Near Coba

G. and I are weighing out the pros and cons of different hammocks,
the colour, the strength of the yarn, how many pesos for this or that style.
Across the road a colony of dogs trails behind children riding bicycles,
animals so lean they already haunt us.
By the lake a man throws chicken to an alligator, says this keeps it
    from town,
a stand of seven or eight buildings, dust trails that would be roads.
On the cafe tables bougainvillaea flounders in glass jars, dry as paper
    from the sun.
By the garden wall a young girl shows us a tooth nestled on her palm.
The forest folded over the ruins we have come to see —
    an improbable landscape:
here a tower, here a wall of bound roots, here a mountain's open door.

But what if this only exists for us now? The breeze off the lake,
    the bright feather
of the forest floor, the children's laughter carried from the village?
And if, when we leave, it will be forgotten, folded back into the hand
    of memory,
memory who thought *bird* and made a bird, who thought *water* and made
    a stream.
G. and I thinking *a small village outside of Coba* and a hammock stand

and the weave of those hammocks, hung like nets from the rafters above.
The smell of fried eggs, the sound of the dogs padding softly
     down the trails,
the clang of a bicycle bell, the tentative flap of a bird's wings —
all of it temporal and extravagant. A tooth in the hand once rooted.
     Ruins
transformed into a city before turning back into ruins again.

Enter Anywhere, Reply to Anything

The days collapse one into the other like folding chairs
and I am nowhere. Tied to the act of giving myself away.
Even iconography held loosely: books, dishtowel, light
blue dress; child, children, flowers in a crystal vase.

A diagram of excess. The lavender outside the door
bolting out of the ground again. The paraphrase of the wind.
Hours, rehearsing 'evening.' Counting what I would withhold
from anyone. A catalogue of how little is nailed down.

So, let anyone enter the story.

A man on horseback riding through the K— valley,
a girl at a window in a muslin gown. Whole histories walking
sideways to this encounter, to the stopped clock on the sill,
bowl of green apples, jug of milk. All the usual trappings.

Greetings, he says, and bows.
And she says *hello*.

Notice how the beginning is *Once* and never *Always*.
It's never the same two trees embroidered against
the same blank sky. Though every hour is equal,
every girl at a window a prelude to *yes*.

And so I often go back to the line in the story that says:
*My life then for a number of years was spent
in aggravating silly details —*
and sometimes refuse to read on.

Imagine that kind of weather: the valley quiet and the
horseman stopping. Two hundred pages of *mist billowing
out of the gorges*. A convalescence. How it stays
the trees. Refuses the wind's desire to move them.

Art as Evidence, Auschwitz

When they unlocked the doors,
Brought in a lamp.
When the boarded windows were opened,
The walls torn down,

What they found was art,
And not the art of ruin —
A building splayed apart, the reduction
That is base geometry —

What they found was pen and ink,
The improbability of watercolour,
Sketches of the dead hidden in the walls
And a landscape: Bielsk in Autumn.

They found the variable that is memory:

Yellowed paper, old canvas,
A girl with a ribbon in her hair drawn on a
Square of paper so small, that rolled up,
It resembled a cigarette, nothing more.

Here and there the attempt
To remember exactly:
> *A Children's Transport*
> *The Barrack Entrance*
> *Clothes Hanging On a Bunk Bed*

Or an oak table, wood chair, the glint
Of light through a window,
The absolute value of, the degree of, the mass of
Tomatoes on a sill, ripening in the sun.

And what if they'd found nothing?
If the building had been razed?
> *The Dead Cart*
> *The Vaulted Hallway*
> *The Jew with a Yellow Star and a Book on His Knees*
Burned or lost to the wind or taken?

But art, its evidence, endures.
Hung in a room where those who made the work
Can be remembered:
He was ten, it was three days before his next birthday;
> *the Vistula had flooded its banks.*

What are we left with in such a room?
The fractus of history?
The last ash on the wind?
A variable that reduces down beyond measure?

That much?
Maybe nothing?
Maybe more.

Barriers, in Six Parts

I

A wall: stone, mud, brick, mortar.
Any barricade so high we can't see
over it. Can only call out to the other side,
enquire after the weather. *Is it cold,*
Captain Scott? Does the ice still crack underfoot
as it did then?

II

Refusal: the words *no, never, I will not.*
Scott's abhorrence at being asked
to turn back. Any word indicating sheer
implausibility. The way we speak in negatives
after a war. The addition of the word *again.*
The sound the body makes while dying.
The writer eyeing his second to last sentence.
The final foothold coming over the wall.

III

Landscapes: forests, valleys, oceans, deserts,
any great divide. *Ku-to-yen* in Pound's poem
"The River Merchant's Wife: a Letter."
All those places that reel into the distance
like unending scrolls. The perfect calligraphy
of mountains. Anywhere man has never set foot.
Anywhere man has set foot but never left.
Scott's tent flap on the far side of the crevasse
lifting like a page in a novel. *Denouement —*
a wall that drops down to the sea.

IV

The body: how we sit inside it impatient
as bees in a jar. The spark of intention,
heart thumping against the chest as if testing
the strength of its walls. How one night,
before leaving his wife, Scott counted
the number of places their bodies touched
while sleeping. Believing that even if he survived,
they would never fit together that way again.
The thin parchment that is skin,
how we sometimes want to walk out of it,
leave it like an old coat at the edge of a lake,
and formless, dive in.

V

Language: the absolute failure of conveyance.
The infinite variety of *stone*. Whether we picture it
sitting in our hands or as part of a mountain.
Whether its edges are hard or round.
The loose paraphrase of words like *sorrow*.
Countries where *death* and *dying* mean the same thing.
Noga, in a Northern tongue, signifying *leg* and *foot*,
ruka meaning *arm* and *hand*. Scott halfway to the Pole
thinking he'd become indivisible from the great
inland plateau. That he stretched on forever, would never
be so small as to sit in his body again.
The wall of an unnamed glacier in front of him,
anchored like an enormous question,
the answer to which he did not know.

Time: temperament and patience. Hours
that spool away like a length of film.
Dickens filling pages upon pages with the elaborate
description of a suit, the slow detail of buttons.
Satellites blinking hundreds of times in space
while we read about an old brown pair of shoes.
The river merchant's wife saying *for ever and for ever
and for ever* as if she could reach out and touch
constancy, cup it in her hand like a plum.
Scott eyeing the South Pole with a similar desire —
to walk beyond the body's *no* and stay there,
to test his limits and to put those thoughts
down in a letter, to etch his questions
on a landscape of loss. *All things considered,
the weather is fine here*. That voice, short note,
trailing over the wall at last.

II.

THE PROGRESS

OF HISTORY

We are born with the dead:
See, they return, and bring us with them.

— T.S. Eliot, *Four Quartets*

What Might Have Been

There was a woman at Alexandria named Hypatia, daughter of the
philosopher Theon, who made such attainments in literature and science
as to far surpass all the philosophers of her own time.
— Socrates Scholasticus, *Ecclesiastical History*

We were many factions then, and again divisible.

    I would like to say it rained.

The crowd came roaring past me, then turned.

There was a leaf in my hair. Perhaps it marked me.

In the Caesareum they quartered my body with shells.

    It seemed to go on and on, the wavering.

I was a script of blood, dropped shawl on marble.

Everything edged into infinity, there was a kind of music.

Later, I imagined the act undone, a ribbon moving backwards,

    the body sewn together by grief.

A trick of philosophy, dome of the imagination.

Bruises turned to pearls, pearls weeping into skin.

Alchemy. Even the text unwritten.

    What might have been is an abstraction —

Trees stitched along the avenue awaiting procession.

Fountains, gardens, temples, a barrack-state.

The acorn in the husk of its universe.

    That it may outlive us all.

Know more than we do.

Between Un-being and Being

The cross-beam of the Shinto gateway is without any curve ... The shrine-fence is not painted red nor is the Shrine itself roofed with cedar shingles ...

— Saka, *Diary of a Pilgrim to Ise*, 1342

Let's define the world by what it is not.

    Treasure in all forms.

A rice field that becomes a trove of stumps.

In the middle, the memory of trees.

Toward the Kushida: eulalia bushes, thickets.

    What is true, changes.

Villagers have cleansed themselves here for centuries;

The practical is also sacred.

The temple gate has fallen, but can be raised in the mind.

    In the cleft *between un-being and being*.

The administration cares little for the torii,

But it does not matter, their ignorance will be reborn.

Many have met an otherworldly man in this place.

    I am old and may not return.

Some argue that the verses are all we have.

How once, all was Darkness,

Until a great mirror was cast in the heavens,

    strung with jewels.

And hung on Mount Kagu with blue and white cloth.

And Do Not Call it Fixity

*King Henry, then being apprised of this, and because the passage of the
river at Blangy, in Ternois, was long and narrow, before crossing it, made six
noblemen of his vanguard divest themselves of their coats of mail and cross first to
see whether the passage had no guard.*

— Jehan de Wavrin, *A French Knight's Account*, The Battle of Agincourt, 1415

It begins at the river, a hare's bones lapped clean.

    The sky yielding to the trees.

I let go my armour as charged by the King,

Ford the water in the folds of my tunic,

Stand on the far bank in the flayed light, heaving.

    Where do the faces come from?

The cornfield, a hundred bannerless poles.

The stones in the river bed, round polished skulls.

Bright things ebbing into darkness —

    Trumpets, gauntlets.

We have turned circles, passed ourselves.

Days dull and never ending. The finest of our lives.

Seed-bed of history, we skirt the elements.

    And do not call it fixity, the bright chimes of steel,

The slick field, the carrion call, wielding.

We are entering the annals of victory.

Will lay down our armour when it is done.

    Return to another river, cross over.

Find ourselves at the mouth of such a place again.

The World Moves in Appetency

Here also are yet standing the ruins of the old Tower of Babel, which,
being upon a plain ground, seemeth afar off very great; but the nearer you come to
it, the lesser and lesser it appeareth.

— John Eldred, Babylon 1583

In the desert all matter becomes linear,

     Else you would go mad, circle the heat for years.

I have been to the brown depths of the map.

The body a burial shroud, sack of leather,

Dead wick of a candle drifting between dunes.

     We keep to what shadow we find.

In the distance, temples small as clay jars.

The world's half-life, fountains of sand, all scale flown.

Everything a burnished copper, lost between the past

     and an equidistant future.

The way I sometimes imagine myself a cloak on a hook —

All that sustained me gone:

Church bells, banquets, a spoon delighting a glass of wine.

     The vibration of being.

The desert a curtain. Sandbox. Flyleaf.

Shimmering like the goldfish in the manor pond.

And so *the world moves in appetency,*

     one eye to the surface,

The unwritten passage begging us on.

Caught in the Form of Limitation

According to my promise, I send you what I observed of the solar eclipse,
though I fear it will not be of any great use to you. I was not prepared with any
instruments for measuring time, or the like ...

— William Stuckeley, 1724

The fields fold into blue evening, but it is not evening.

    The valley dims, becomes ocean;

The grass, waves. Horses swim in the hollow.

Sheep gather in the hull of their pens.

The latitudes, graze.

    The sun an apple God pares with a blade.

All of us held in a pocket, *caught in the form of limitation*,

And carried down a dark hall.

It seemed the universe had swept the attic of the sky.

    Children under a blanket — how mythology begins.

Gods who invent a world by blinking. A lamplighter,

Late for work one evening, can only reach one globe at a time.

Existence a force of will. So too, illumination.

    The bright penny I once kept in a jar.

The sun a treasure chest slowly opened,

Bright Spanish coins, glittering jewels.

And now a field where there was an ocean.

    The animals wild-eyed,

As if they imagine we could blow such a candle out.

Here, Or There, Or Elsewhere

Yesterday I went for the second time to the Crystal Palace ... It seems as if only magic could have gathered this mass of wealth from all ends of the earth — as if none but supernatural hands could have arranged it thus ...
— Charlotte Brontë, *The Great Exhibition*, 1851

Chandeliers, musical instruments, clocks, bright things.

    The clack and hum of machinery.

By the fountain a man moving lightly across a highwire.

The delicacy of his pacing. A solitude.

It is as if we are all inside a great glass bell,

    and he, the chime, up there wavering.

Swans in a raised pond, carriages in the shapes of swans.

Are we in the natural world or is it in us?

Lions on a grassy plain tucked into a box of jewelry.

    The world gathering at the platform of a busy station.

Progress lifting her chin: *I am here, or there, or elsewhere.*

Everywhere children burrowing into their mother's skirts,

Small ivory globes in carved wood stands.

    We are all these things: trinkets, lace, spoons, ephemera,

Stamps drifting off the edges of letters.

Wonder a private thing, high-ceilinged. A transept filled with harps.

And also a quiet. The hush of possibility.

    The sound of the woods at the start of a fable.

So many birds we have never seen.

The Poetry Does Not Matter

Considering the enormous economic dislocation which the war operations
have caused in the regions where the campaign is raging, there seems to be very
little corresponding disturbance in the bird life of the same districts.
— H.H. Munro, *Birds on the Western Front*, 1916

The sparrow hawk has steady nerves and has not left us.

    Days, the shapes drawn in the sky equal writing.

The crows have left the Front. The barn owl remains.

Magpies nest in the shell-swept earth.

Mice frenzy in the trenches.

    The world in miniature.

What we know of permanence: omens gusting,

Harbingers, the stuttered morning call.

Poplars reduced to needles that compass our eyes to the sky.

    That every bird might come back here.

That the world *resume*, orchards recall their fruit.

Days I see myself from a height, less real than the weather.

A dead branch flogged by wind.

    It seems we will be here forever: skylark, meadow,

The chaffinch's chipped notes, staccato telegrams.

We are already dead to them. Fences grown dull and familiar.

The poetry does not matter. We are, each of us, a word.

    For what gathers sets out and does not return:

Hope. A rook song.

Fare Forward, Voyagers

Voyager 1 and Voyager 2 continue their current mission to study the region in space where the Sun's influence ends and the dark recesses of interstellar space begin.

— NASA, *http://voyager.jpl.nasa.gov*, 2003

Beyond the blue gate, beyond the river,

     You are farther away than anything we've touched.

Purse of greetings, aperture of hope, carrier of bird song.

A blinking eye reeling through space,

Acorn, bellwether.

     And like Brendan on his voyage —

Antennas for oars — you push into the wake storm.

And we are the ghosts that follow, a necklace of stars.

Yes, *fare forward, voyagers,*

     The end of known space could be anything:

A desert stretched between galaxies,

Darkness dusted, pearls of sand. A lighthouse.

Or the absence of comparison,

     so purely itself it can't be framed.

Or, maybe the end of what's known is a kind of humming.

The echo of everything we've said and done,

Have yet to do,

     out there,

drifting between shores.

III.

PUBLIC RECORDS,

LOCAL HISTORIES

Attempts to Know the Present

All day, matter drifts.

G. and I in the piazza on a bright pinwheel
        of an afternoon,
under the stuttering light of an oak tree.

A kineograph that becomes a girl
        lowering a bucket down four storeys
to her sister on the street below.

That delicate hand-over-hand balance,
        whole minutes winnowed into *meanwhile*,
the bucket's sway, its litter of fine white eggs,

                bright pinions of *during*.

Tell me how to understand the present,
        the spell of bees in the box flowers, the swinging
skirt of a white towel's shadow.

I've spent whole days searching for a point of intersection,
        a letter-hedged *now*,
the corded seam of a book, the clasp

that holds the reliquary,

    the middle note in last night's concerto,
and that note's own dark quaver,

        the brow of an unremarkable door.

In the Museo di Scienza, between astrolabes and pendulums:
    Galileo's finger — rolled scroll of bone,
compass needle — points mutely toward the sky.

And I go backward again:
    the objective lens, the *Dialogues*, the clack
of an eggshell tapping the bucket rim.

G. says that, undone, Galileo's finger
    becomes its own measurement
of the mean motions of time.

        But I say this finger is a poem —

That it desires language.
    To open a book to any page
and hold it down.

Marginalia Found in Books at the Vancouver Public Library

In T.S. Eliot's *Collected*, a handwritten dedication,
       To all self-worshippers.

Over the line in Lord Nelson's letter to Lady Hamilton
       where he confesses,
"I can neither Eat or Sleep for thinking of You my dearest love,
       I never touch even pudding ..."
AM loves JB, looped letters in fat pencil.

In a cookbook, recipes corrected,
       an even hand that writes in blue pen,
They're wrong about the eggs.

In Heraclitus, Japanese kanji drawn lightly beside a fragment
       on the boundaries of the soul —
a bird house with an open roof for *journey*,
a woman's long skirt-train for *road*.

In Walter Benjamin's essays, a question mark
       after the word "civilization."

By the account of "An Albatross Shot on 1 October 1719,"
       the comment *It could not have happened this way.*

       Only once, when I was young,
       did I write in a book not my own —

In the *Collected Works of Emily Dickinson*,
    with a black-ink pen from my father's study

I noted:

    it's death, dear Emily,
        with a small "d."

Mishaps in Childhood (from the Calendar of Coroner's Rolls, 1301–37)

Mischance: The pathway clear. To either side, trees. A forest.

To have heard the sough wind. To desire shade. To be curious.
To step off the rut of the road and into oblivion.

The evolution of "accident." Five children: *A lost ball; A game
on the way to school; A ruse; A distraction; Playing on the timber pile.*

*In the hour of prime. On the Feast of St Philip. After the hour
of vespers. On nineteen, July. In the ward of Vintry.*

*Was in the house. Was playing in the street. Was walking across
London Bridge. Was riding a white horse. Was carried to the shop.*

Died of the fall. Of the blow. Drowned.

*Lingered until the Friday before the Feast of Saint Margaret.
Lingered until the next day. Lingered until the hour of curfew.*

Aged three years.
Eight years.
Seven.
Five.
No age given.

Look: the carefully ravelled years. The verge of possibility.
The woods still dark and cool.

(Somewhere the sough of wind. Animals in the trees. A voice calling.
Somewhere a hawk circling.)

Look: the spool of an eye unwinding.

The son of. The son of. The son of. The daughter of. The son.

On hearing this. Being asked. Were told. Afterwards. Giving way.

Anyone. Anyone. (Was noted. As recorded.) Anyone, at all.

Factory Conditions c. 1815: A Female Millhand Responds to Parliamentary Commissioners

What age are you?
Twenty-three.

(In the garden of my youth, a spindle.
Some have on them the faintest trace
of flowers, a steady room. I am all chaff
and threshing, needle thin, misery worked
into bone.)

Where do you live?
At Leeds.

(An ivy-rimmed cup filled with tea. As if
such gardens exist — those bolts of green
on the outskirts of the city. There is no
colour here, we are in need of dusting.
Though I often imagine an elsewhere,
bright scarves waving from windows.)

When did you begin work at the factory?
When I was six years old.

(Days my mother would set a slice of bread
in a bowl of gravy, then wrap it in cloth,
bundle it under my arm.
Twice I was caught chewing on the cloth

for marrow. And despite hunger, have
never done it again.)

What kind of mill is it?
Flax mill.

(Once I heard it called 'linum' and for an hour
the work sang, became a hat with spun flowers,
bright knots bobbing under high ceilings.
It's said the factory roof is covered in grass,
above us wild flowers at the whim of the weather;
all that fainting and recovering in the wind.)

What was your business in that mill?
I was a little doffer.

(A hand. As if the body does not exist.
I have scutched and heckled. I have set the frames
and emptied them. I stop the spindle and the world
spins down. Who would ask for anything?
Voices lifted like skirt hems. I know questions
exist — see them handed to the men sometimes,
like cards on a platter.)

Suppose you flagged a little or were late, what would
    they do?
Strap us.

(My mother once pulled me through the market
by my hair. A clump of it in her hand, unspun threads
lining her palm. This was still an act of love:
a blanket in the making, the first thin cords of a warm
sweater. Which, if she had the means, or hope,
I know she'd have tried to mend.)

    Where are you now?
    In the poorhouse.

(Knees and ankles ruined, back bent into a hook,
I am all question. Head hanging like a cane over an old man's
wrist. The manager here once offered me a tuppence
to be his footstool. It was not so far to the ground.
So I crawled into myself further, called out
low enough now? then took his foot.)

A Last Letter from Your Most Affectionate, Anon

I thought you would have been in the country before this time,
    the Manor is lonely without you.

I regret the gazebo but not what followed there —

Blame the landscape gardner,
    his shaded walks, pared views,

And the willow that fans the lake temple;
    folly after folly.

The half seen thing
    a snare that baits us with desire —

The maid bringing a tray when I was a girl,
    a glimpse of the sweetness it carried.

Come down by the Sturbridge horse carrier
    who lyes at the Castle Wood streete this Sunday,

His Lordship is away and the grounds
    need mending.

At night the stable boy walks out with a lamp
    to feed the caged birds in the far garden.

From my window I follow his light into darkness
     and think of you.

In the morning gold cages thimble the beech
     as I walk through the flower breaches,

The birds sing for me,
     and I think of you.

Perhaps my last message miscarried
     Or the woodstock at the edge of the lake

No longer pleases you.

You have taken the Measure of me,
     altered the sway of the trees.

The brace of a month, a great unkindness.

Everyday a procession to the window,
     an hour at the piano,

Acting in Form a counterpoint
     to weeping.

I play for no one.

This morning I heard the hunting dogs
      go out with the servants,

The kitchen floors trammelled
      when the men returned with game.

A hare hung over Gede's shoulder,
      unremarked upon and tossed on the larder table.

For an hour I've stood in the doorway
      studying its fell neck —

as if there is life in it yet —
      And think of you.

Ernst Mach On Wonder

Said with certainty to a crowded hall on a November evening —

That the element of wonder never lies in the phenomenon itself,
but always in the person observing.

Twilight. And after the lecture, a late dinner.
Three of them walking through Stare Mesto and along Vaclaus street.
The sound of a piano in an apartment above,
Schumann perhaps, no one in the party can say for sure,
but together they listen to the notes drift and settle,
small icicles from the eaves dropping into snow.

Burton and Speke making their way to Lake Tanganyika
at that same minute, four-thousand miles away.
Verdi's *La Forza del Destino* premiering in St. Petersburg.
The continent's first bicycle race ending in Paris.
Whole parts of the world awake, other parts sleeping.

A wildflower in a stranger's window glimpsed
through ice-encrusted glass. The improbable yellow of its petals.
The distortion of form like a faraway lamp.
Mach, considering the relationship between the body
and all other matter in the universe. Nothing less than that.

The restaurant, busy. An argument underway in the back room.
The hostess greeting the men from behind the bar.
A couple near the window almost touching hands.
The inexplicable smell of cloves.

Elsewhere steamers churn their way across the Atlantic,
horse-drawn trams clatter through London fog.
Elsewhere the first line of Turgenev's *Fathers and Sons*
is read aloud in a private library — *A gentleman in the early forties,*
wearing check trousers and a dusty overcoat, came out on to the low porch
of the coaching-inn on the — highway.

To reject speculation. To understand the difference between
one kind of illumination and the next. The candle on the table,
the rose glow of his companions as they take off their overcoats,
settle into chairs. The lamp light refracted in the cutlery,
in the pure white of an eye.

The drinks arrive. The fire in the corner grows bright.
A woman in the most extraordinary shade of blue walks by.
The world lulled into contentment so that even the perfume
of the restaurant owner's daughter becomes a colour,
a glimpse of violet as she leans in to pour the wine.

Leper Colony, D'Arcy Island

He lost the word for *hand*
because of the hand's absence.
Instead he says *hut*, *boat*,
garden. He says
this unforgiving weather.

His is a culture of men
abandoned with food and coffins,
a few sheafs of paper,
though they have no desire
to write anything down.

He tilts the soup bowl
to his mouth with his wrists,
as strenuous an exercise
as rowing, as using his shoulder
to hoe and weed hard earth.

The boat comes once each season
like a ghost across Haro Strait,
the men standing on the beach
or carried down on litters
to be counted.

I am here and *I am here,*
they call, and *here I am.*
Take our names back
to the city and say them.

Island, tree, hut, hole, grave,
they have their own language,
words they will and won't say,
a preference for nouns
over questions.

How long before they lose
more than the word for *hand*?
How long before the winter?
The false reprieve of spring?

In the oldest hut a man
of fifty-three, who can't find
the word for *heart,*
or *happiness,* or *home.*

The End of the War

The year you were born women killed their children
when they learned their husbands were dead
then gave themselves up to the same dark eye; the war
finally over, confetti in the streets, Mussolini strung up
in Piazza Loreto, Hitler dead in Berlin.
SS soldiers blowing themselves up to avoid surrender.
Everywhere broken skin on fists, collapsed buildings,
the abstract of bodies that are no longer
bodies, that become the grey webbing of dreams.

In those days there wasn't anything humans couldn't do —
raze a city, stall time, kill what it was we once gave life to.
The stopped clock in the city square told us nothing,
the house that stood on the edge of obliteration swayed once,
then gave in. The wind that crossed the continent circled the globe
carrying death's ashes, then came back to us again.

Still, in the slack of all that dying, in the fierce distension
of birth, something endured. You saw the world differently.
For you it hung like a sturdy door. This room leading to
        that room
and on to the next. The sound of your cry coming back
with a soft answer. The distance between you and pure possibility,
as navigable as a finger running over a map. And the future?
The span of time that follows night. The brightness of those
first few hours of morning.

Village Books

Before it was a root cellar it was a hole in the earth —
under a mat, in the corner of the room.
Three books placed in its keep, then buried,
the only three books in the village —
Li Po's *Collected Works* and two historical fictions:
Peach Blossom Fountain, The Three Kingdoms.

> *In the third month the town of Hsien-yang*
> *Is thick-spread with a carpet of fallen flowers.*

A scroll of willow etchings, the record player,
Prokofiev and Gao Ming's "Lute Song" hidden under
the beating hooves of ponies at the far end of the field,
then covered with straw and dung.

> *Who in Spring can bear to grieve alone?*
> *Who, sober, look on sights like these?*

The animals know nothing. In the pasture, sheep,
like small white pages, drift in the wind.
Sorrel ponies amble up to the gate for grain,
then canter off, nearly pulling the music from the ground.

> *Riches and poverty*, Li Po wrote, *long or short life.*
> As if these are our only choices.

When the seasons change what object will I be holding
in my hands? And how will it speak of my crimes,
my education? Ink well? Eyeglass? Flute? It doesn't matter.
The burning effigy in the city square is also me.

A thousand horses, red banners, an army sent
like locusts through a village — it's rarely that kind
of revolution. Often it's simply a man in a peasant jacket
who comes and knocks on the door. Who stands there
patiently while it opens, expecting to be welcomed,
invited in.

The Gorilla Cages, Dublin Zoo

All those years living in this city and not once
did I visit the zoo.
Skirted it certainly, had picnics in Phoenix Park,
but averted my eyes
even at the signs leading to:
The Wild Heart of Africa, Primate Pavilion.

So I nod at you,
now that we are both visitors to this city,
surveying a strange asylum
each from our own side of the glass.

The woman beside me tapping her umbrella
against the pane.
Once, twice, three times,
until she is rattling the partition.
Both of us wide-eyed at the commotion.
Wondering: What kind of loneliness
brings a person
to do that?

And So the Country is Changing

Driving to Sligo one summer,
I saw five men in a curragh
hunkered down on the grass
in a roundabout
where the N17 meets the N15
to Donegal,
before veering north again
to the West Country and the sea.

Nowhere to stop for miles,
no place to seek cover,
just five men in a curragh
dropped from the sky
or lifted by a nefarious God
from a river
to row over the clover,
the wind against them,
their oars dry.

Absolute Objects

I want to write *desk*.

To allow for *carpet*, *dog*, a *half empty cup of coffee*, the *clock*, the *almanac*,
       pocket guides,

the *Book of the Century*.

To offer *red shirt*, *faded jeans*, *socks with holes*. *Four pairs of black shoes*
       in the corner.

And *door*, *lock*, *chain*, *window*, *bower of lavender*, *rose bush*, the *dog's bones*,
       autumn.

I want to say *I have been sad for days and have not left the house*.

To state *the mail arrived*.

But this afternoon everyday facts slip into the past
the way Renaissance landscapes recede into a single mote of grey —
poplars reduced to nothing,
ochre skies reeled into a last fleck of night.

In Sligo, it was *radiance*.

The coast a pearl ribbon that met the bay, the moth-light of the moon.

Farmer's dogs bounding in from back fields to chase me down the road,
one after the other, like a relay.

Each dog leaving off at his property line so the next dog could take over.

The last escorting me as far as the cemetery, his high bark flung
into the bowl of the sea.

I have never been so sure of anything in my life —
those dogs, the sea,
fixed edges of darkness,
that country.

Here, there is *antique glass, rain, a mirror.*
There are *unopened letters on the table.*
Absolute objects.
The borders of feeling.

There are those who could do more with this, who might see
blackcaps warbling in the afternoon, apples giving themselves to the ground.
The *skirt tails of summer.* The *fine tuning of the seasons.*
Oak leaves trembling like violin strings. Whole symphonies gusting in the maple.

But what I know sits outside the frame of things —
A strange dog waiting around the bend.
The low note of the wind.
And beyond that again, a cemetery.
Long grass. Iron gates. The hush of memory.
And my body curled like a shell in the long arms of the sea.

The Natural History Museum, Dublin

I've failed them before —
whole canopies of bird life stalled,

the sleek winter of their wings,
trace of dust covering.

Days I cannot name them, imagine
the pitch of their call.

And like the dead and their
long staircases,

I forget that flight is also
a kind of climbing.

My face reflected a hundred times
in a hundred glass eyes

so that even the lark's stillness
is about me.

Here, pearl-coloured moths
are tacked in glass boxes,

two foxes stand in parched grass,
ears empty of wind.

Here, deer turn in the middle
of a staged wandering

to fix their sights
on a distant field.

The bodies of the dead made beautiful
because they do not *want*.

What matters in the end is that
I always come here and get it wrong:

Wonder is not only the bird in flight
but also its gliding shadow.

Failure, indifference
what passes between.

Pin in the heart,
the eye pried open.

Categories of Loss

Misplaced words, words that hang around our necks like empty lockets.
The tribe that forgot the word for *thumb*. Or the silversmith
in the Marquez novel, who watched *anvil* dissipate into nothing.

Objects, touchstones. The wedding photo of my mother with confetti
in her palm. A scrap of marble from Venice. A fossil. What falls away,
becomes outdated: old shoes, summer hats, memory.

Offerings, acts of petition. Knees touching a wood beam. The farmer
in spring, who gives the first seed to the wind. The grave maintained,
the stone garden, the threshed heart. Custom.

Annals of instruction etched in dead languages —

> *To supplicate the Storm-God ...*
> *To anoint the general and his battle gear ...*
> *To win the beloved ...*
> *To end bad dreams ...*

Ritual, the circumambulation of *hope*. Climbing a ladder to find another
ladder. Going back to the thousand unsaid things to pull them from
the river. The flicker of language, how it changes in our hands.

Love, in its possessive, a stone in the mouth, fragment of a larger idea.
Amulets, promise rings, photographs: how we pin things down.
The grief we feel knowing that what we keep will leave us.

History, a loose match cast into darkness. Elaboration, a blue ribbon
on a dress. Or the long hall of a great house, whose ghosts
try all the doors. A hundred covered lamps and shadows.

> *What lantern in the dark then?*
> *What word to light it?*

IV.

OLD NOTEBOOKS

Everything Lost is Found Again

the ring that lay for months behind the dresser,
the book finally returned by a friend,

apples reborn in the boughs of an old tree
and the years appearing suddenly

ripe fruit in the open hand.

The Story as I See It

If I say, my arms cast out in this southern exposure,
this is all we have for making: sudden grace or lack thereof,
the skin that covers us in its thinness, a flush
that starts high on the cheekbones, a span of warm hands,

this is all of it, our tenacity, the stripped-down caravan
we found in a field, the pillowcase we hung across the broken window,
the floor coming up in the kitchen.
And like a book already written we consider how to hold memory

in the mouth. We hang our heels over the lowest slat of the gate
and swing, looking as far down the road as we can.
This is what I know of transience: that you will never see me
this way again, that the light will touch the leaves of the alder tree

this way only once, that we cast ourselves out of the past
like human cannonballs because of the darkness behind us.
But listen, there is music, and the steady thread of our breathing.
Even here, in this place, miles from anywhere.

On Love Poems

I'd like to write a poem in which
the hero with the lazy eye
falls close to love with a woman
standing under a stop sign
in the worst kind of weather,

falls close to love with the outline
of ordinary thighs under a rain-soaked
skirt, his eye sidling up
towards her ample waist,
plain face and her hat, worn

at an awkward angle. And I would like
the hero to come toward her,
step in a puddle as he crosses the road,
and I would like the whole
of the blemished world to cease

existing between them: the pocked
concrete sidewalk, the whorled
knots of the trees, the nail holes
in the telephone poles, the crevices
and cuts — smoothed over.

Then I would like storybooks rewritten
to reflect the fact that no one is whole,
the endings left wide open, the possibility
of loss always there, hanging
like a street light.

We think we know the world and imagine
there is order to it, but this turning
the corner into love is as much a myth
as anything — the man with the lazy eye
and the women who walks by him.

Still, what astounds me most in this
isn't our tireless wanting, the old
college try. It isn't the half-life
we try not to fall into. It's
how we find each other

remarkable, despite the absence
of wisdom or humour or pity, despite
the absence of attributes we cannot name.
All of us wanting just enough and searching
the pockets of the world to find it.

On Adultery Poems

I don't imagine it the way they do,
the husk of a lie, falling back into oneself
with bitterness, acrimony, the cold eye
that studies the self undressing
like a young girl practicing in a mirror.

Let's say it isn't all self-hating morbidity,
happy people drawn to the one thing
that could easily undo them: all those
rows gone wrong in winter cabins, in bedrooms,
in the quiet domestic of the kitchen.

Let's refrain from using words like *destroy*,
from adding *marriage*, *happiness*, *trust*, *integrity*
like a train to the grammar. Let's put down
Karenina and stop thinking about trains.
Truth is a tricky constellation.

All around us planets whirl on wobbly trajectories,
whole stars give in to dark matter,
list a minute on the cusp of something bigger,
waver in the preposition of a telescope,
before *whoosh* they're gone.

Maybe loss is fidelity too, and maybe
there is bright honesty in the flux of that wavering.
Like an idea that goes back and forth in one's mind:
should I, *shouldn't I* and *what if*,
before it all gets tipped over, *I do*?

But what do I know? I can't even be faithful
to this poem. Have made it, in my own way,
to please you. The confessional *I*,
the sly imperative *don't*, the perilous
declarative *imagine*.

Thesis Statement on the Matter of our Relationship

Odysseus at sea does not interest me. All that
floundering, the near near drownings,

His inability to settle on which of a thousand
waves to crash under.

I like his stillness. Stranded on Kalypso's island
groaning and breaking his heart for sorrow —

As if sorrow was its own briny wave,
distance, the scarred face of the moon.

Penelope in her room worlds away, whole essays
of birds, their complex migrations, between them.

His days spent on shore studying the cordage of a leaf.
Turning it over until its rigging breaks in his hands.

Epics are easy.
All lash and fury. Entreaty.

We, too, desire to ask. To gain favour with the gods.
But we will not last. Will sit in the long stretch

Between the eye and landfall forever,
wade through all that is unsteady and slow.

Odysseus wanting only to sail home to the smell
of his woman's hair, to be caught in the net of it —

A ballast we can only imagine: Ithaca's groves
and temples, the cleft lips of its rivers.

That port, not as far away as Odysseus might think.
A distance he could bridge with a lance,

His love a barbed message sent across the water,
and Penelope right where he wants her —

Taking in his gift; the pause in the grieving,
that marks her as his.

Things You Would Ask For

for M.

Things you would ask for if you had the chance —

Food for everyone

Good wine

Worldwide pax mobiscum

Your mother's lemon meringue pie

To remember the name of that one song
off that old album

To revisit the winter in Winnipeg when you
kissed Donna Bogaski under the bleachers
after giving her your gloves

Those gloves — a gift from your father

For the right word to manifest itself
when called upon

And regular, modest miracles —

A parking spot in front of the house
where you've been invited for Christmas dinner

Raccoons that leave the garbage bins alone

A son brought back from the dead
long enough for you to hold him

A holiday in the Lake District

Oranges imported from Spain.

Small things, easily given.

Practice, Or, The Storms

The storms that winter were fierce —
cars stalled in the middle of town
or swerved into banks of snow and
people abandoned them, walked blindly
through the sleight of hand that was the weather.

That was the year my parents kept
skidoo suits and a spare battery in the trunk.
The year the snow lasted into spring,
everything bathed and clean come summer.

That was also the year my neighbour's mother
sat down in a whiteout and died.
Her body uncovered two days later, under drifts
at the foot of the oak tree in her yard.

That spring, school lessons took on new meanings —
the location of the heart, latitude,
how perspective allows a painter to find
a landscape's centre. Subtraction, division,
continued attempts at the cursive 'I.'

For months I saw her everywhere —
in the cereal aisle of the supermarket,
on the stretch of highway that heads out of town.
Curled up and lightly breathing
at the foot of every tree.

This, how I learned to turn tragedy
over in my hands, examine it from all sides,
like a gift hidden in tissue and ribbon. How I
imagined opening it again and again,
to find something that was mine.

Genesis, Or, Tornado, Essex County

First, the pebble-strewn shoulder, hail of gravel
and then the pickup, skidding on two wheels,
heads into the gully, mud wash,
the slow torque of steel, axle twisting into a high note,
a last gambol before we upped and rolled
into the corn field, its fluttering
husks like banners on the windshield,
the dust a ticker-tape parade —

     and my sister still holding the wheel.

The front window blown out by the applause
of five thousand whipped stalks and one
torpedoed can of pop.
My sixth grade science book wedged
above the dashboard like a trophy.

The twister's low whistle all around us then,
a Hank Williams song streeling
through the cassette,

     and somewhere, somewhere
in another field: wood fences splitting and lifting
behind a trail of furrowed earth.
The engine ticking evenly
under the bent hood before us.

And in my hair —
and in my hair —
and in my hair —
and in my hair —
a slip
of paper
from the floor.
An old note
written
in pencil —

    This, how memory works.

Watching the Leonids in November

G. and I alone in a clearing,
on a drop sheet in the freezing cold,
three sweaters each, toques and gloves.
The dog running back and forth
into the woods while the sky did nothing.

It's a joke between us, how I have spent
years of my life waiting
for fabulous things to happen. How
I always want to pack it in just before they do.

So there we were. The same old night sky
promising us a magic trick, holding out
its palms for show. One black glove
and then another and finally,
bright beads of light, hurling across them.

How little it takes to move us: the universe
on holiday, skipping stones across a lake,
G. and I on a dock of earth below.

Those long stretches where so little happens
a kind of preparation for what follows:
that first flash of light, the spark
that makes us.

Old Notebooks

A wave of leaves travels across the park —
oak and maple unfurled, a tattered sail
from an old ship.

     And for an instant
the whole park keels against sky, against
the furrow of clouds edging toward noon,

the way I leaned as a child toward
the bright windows of my classroom

     then righted myself again
hauled back into geometry and science,
the lantern slides of history.

Our trouble, wrote Pascal, *is that we can
no longer sit still in a room.* Too impatient
to write our own accounts and consider them.

     But I say, how coved the sky,
how arched the pillars. Give me the bark text
of the birch, barrel vault of the ash,

give me the copsed doorway that is the far
gate of the Green

and I will sit for days —
study the pinhole stars, the fathoms
turning over me.

The Interval

History never evolves but changes.

— historical supposition

And so long as you haven't experienced
this: to die and so to grow,
you are only a troubled guest
on the dark earth.

— Goethe, *The Holy Longing*

And in the middle of all that falls and converges
the lull of time lived, daily duties,

A museum we enter at midnight.

What is less than, greater than, equal to,
the approximation of art?

Veneration, all that's left, the occasional change
of lighting.

Ordinary moments cut from time
and ushered into new rooms,

Half-understood episodes gleaned
from the privy chamber of Now.

In the archives, a thousand photos
that detail our questions.

So ask again: What means the road?
The boulevard of elm?

Whose house are we entering?

Bowles said, "You must watch your universe
as it cracks above your head."

Mine, already in fragment —

That's what happens when you look to the past:
it comes as all kinds of weather.

Think of Goya's etchings, *The Disasters of War*,
his querying titles:

Why?
What More Is There To Do?
Is This What You Were Born For?

Every death awful and ordinary —

The old man who wakes at night to find
he can't breathe,

His wife holding his head in the crook of her arm
as she waits for the ambulance to arrive.

If the annals end everything with a full stop,
what will propel us to exclamation?

The weight of a body in your arms,
the bed sheets falling away?

Or the finger and thumb that circle a wrist
to find the steady thread of *being*.

The ceiling and then the sky, opening and closing.
Thunder, then lighting, then rain.

Maybe the small changes are enough.

Considerations

The act of writing something down. The act of forgetting.

Alphabets inscribed on clay tablets.

Historiography: *the act of studying the act of writing the act down.*

The verb *to be.*

Monastery wares jotted down in the Book of Kells.

Accounts of dogs and horses halved by swords and thrown in
        to Viking burials.

Burials, plural, recorded at sea.

The palm leaf manuscript borne of a forest.

The truce that becomes a massacre.

The man who watches the battle from the dark boscage of the trees.

The act of witness. The negation of 'I.'

Blood money sewn into jackets and corsets.

Envelopes bearing the royal seal.

Code words.

Objects reflected in the mirrors of paintings.

Pascal looking to the far reaches of the night sky, then down at a mite.

Invoices for wood coffins made with removable bottoms
        during the famine.

Letters of Introduction. Letters of Proposal. Letters of Complaint.

Aides-memoires: cowrie shells, wampum belts, the knotted handkerchief.

Correspondence between writers: *to sit for hours with a person
        who feels at home in the hours.*

Sacks of letters in the low holds of ships.

The Yorkshire novelist at the Historical Novel Symposium who
        seems to be saying the *hysterical* novel.

The act of translation.

Camus' repeated use of the diminutive.

Birth certificates of the Disappeared.

Last wills and testaments signed X.

The dull miracles of the later saints.

The novelist revising: *Daylight began to forsake the red-room; it was past four o'clock, and the beclouded afternoon was tending to drear twilight.*

The Shoah survivor describing the last time she saw her father, asking the cameraman if she could just say his name.

The imperative. The declarative. The possessive.

The epigraph. The epitaph.

Short introductions.

Road signs.

The blank space after *Country of Origin.*

The thousand facets of *from.*

The inevitable *to.*

As in *Wandered* into *the night.*

    Went to *find the answer.*

    Looked to *history* to *know.*

Attempts to Know the Future

The clock's winding key and its gallow ribbon,
  a metal ladder against an old barn wall.

  That things beautiful once can go on
  being beautiful —

Music from distant patios, the surprise
  of an instrument I cannot name.

  A gilded anything — the light-tipped
  work of birds, sketches in ornate frames.

The abjuration of self-portrait: *Woman Lying in Bed*,
  Woman with Her Hand on a Window.

  Useless beauty: fancy dresses, impossible hats
  that stop us in doorways.

What then? *The appearance of the world in front of the world?*
  An elsewhere that assembles itself

  like alphabet blocks into the sudden
  swagger of a word.

I hang roses from rafters, it's what I do.
  Rehearse each petal's falling.

And yes, I want to bring you with me,
to not leave anyone behind.

The dusk road between the cemetery and the greenhouse
will still be there,

pollarded trees will grow grace
and we'll etch ivy over everything.

Books have been bound with less:
toad skins, cup handles, corset stays, kid gloves,

the cord that runs from the piano key
to the hammer.

Barthes spoke of the *interstice of bliss*
but I am interested in what comes after —

scars, bone-catacombs, marginalia.
A place that casts no shadow.

Are you still with me?
How can you be?

We are nowhere we have ever been.

Notes

The poem "The Greeks March into the Land of the Taochians" owes a debt to a poem by Jack Gilbert.

The title "Enter Anywhere, Reply to Anything" comes from a line in Arthur Rimbaud's *A Season In Hell*. The line "My life then and for a number of years …" in the same poem is from Dermot Healy's short story "A Family and a Future" in *Banished Misfortune*, Allison and Busby, 1982. The line "mist billowing out of the gorges" is from Mikhail Lermontov's *A Hero of Our Time*.

The majority of the art work cited in "Art as Evidence, Auschwitz" was exhibited at The Block Museum of Art at Northwestern University in 2002.

The title "In this Spinning World, Who Knows Which is Up?" comes from a line in *The Journals of Sylvia Plath*, Anchor Books, 1982.

The poem titles / italicized lines in "The Progress of History" come from T. S. Eliot's *Four Quartets* (Faber and Faber, 1983).

The quote from Lord Nelson's letter to Lady Hamilton in "Marginalia Found in Books at the Vancouver Public Library" comes from a letter dated 29 January–2 February, 1800, collected in *The Faber Book of Letters* (Felix Pryor, Ed) Faber and Faber, 1988.

The italicized lines in "Mishaps in Childhood" are taken from a Calendar of Coroner's Rolls quoted in Edith Rickert's *Chaucer's World*, Oxford University Press, 1948.

The questions and answers in "Factory Conditions c 1815" are excerpted from a report given by Elizabeth Bentley entitled *A Report of Parliamentary Committee on the Bill to Regulate the Labour of Children in Mills and Factories*, 1832. The ideas in parentheses are mine.

The lines "I thought you would have been in the country before this time" and "Come down by the Sturbridge horse carrier..." in "A Last Letter from Your Most Affectionate, Anon" are from a letter from Lord Windsor to Lord Hatton written in 1658. The letter's original content bears no resemblance to the content of this poem. This poem owes a debt to Tom Stoppard's play *Arcadia*.

The Ernst Mach quote "That the element of wonder ..." used in "Ernst Mach on Wonder" is from Penelope Fitzgerald's novel *The Gates of Angels*, Flamingo, 1992.

The Li Po quotes in "Village Books" are from his poem "Drinking Alone By Moonlight."

The title "Absolute Objects" comes from Joseph Brodsky's statement that the true subject of poetry is "absolute objects and absolute feelings."

The annals cited in the poem "Categories of Loss" are slight variations of those found in Hattusas on tablets dated to the 13th c BC.

The line "groaning and breaking his heart for sorrow" in the poem "Thesis Statement ..." is from Chapter V of Homer's *Odyssey*.

The Goethe translation that prefaces "Interval" is by Robert Bly.

In "Considerations" the line "to sit for hours with a person who feels at home in the hours" comes from a letter by Boris Pasternak to Marina Tsvetayeva, found in *Pasternak, Tsevetayeva, Rilke, Letters: Summer 1926*, nyrb, 2001. The line "Daylight began to forsake the red-room ..." in the same poem is from Charlotte Brontë's *Jane Eyre*, Penguin, 1966.

In "Attempts to Know the Future" the line "That things beautiful once can go on being beautiful" comes from Jorge Luis Borges' Charles Eliot Norton Lectures

(Harvard 1967–68) published as *This Craft of Verse*, Harvard University Press, 2000. The line "The appearance of the world in front of the world" is Peter Handke's — though it came to me through Van Morrison's recorded version of Handke's "Song of Being A Child". The book bindings referred to in this poem are those by the Surrealist artist Mary Reynolds. A selection of her work was on display at The Art Institute of Chicago in the spring of 2004.

The quote on "observation" in my acknowledgements is from Sir Arthur Conan Doyle's *Hound of the Baskervilles*.

Finally, this collection owes a debt to Prof. Frederick Holmes' book *The Historical Imagination* a text that inspired me to think about how the tenets of postmodern historical narrative could be applied to poetry.

"Ernst Mach on Wonder" is for Lynn.
"The End of the War" is for Martin.
"Absolute Objects" is for Dermot.
"Everything Lost is Found Again" is for Kerry Ohana.
"The Interval" is for Shaun O'Mara.

Acknowledgments

My gratitude to the Canada Council and the BC Arts Council for financial assistance during the writing of this book. Thanks to my wonderful editor Lynn Henry, to everyone at Polestar / Raincoast and to Carolyn Swayze. Thanks also to Billeh Nickerson for kindly reading through the early drafts of these poems. To Dermot Healy, Patrick Friesen, Esta Spalding and Alison Pick for various and buoying conversations about poetry. To Kerry, Jenise, Tom, Martin and Alma for their friendship. And, as always, to Glenn: "The world is full of obvious things which nobody by any chance ever observes" — in this way, he brings as much to these poems as I do.

About the Author

Aislinn Hunter was born in Belleville, Ontario and lived in Dublin, Ireland before making her home in Vancouver, British Columbia. She has published three critically acclaimed books: *What's Left Us and Other Stories* (finalist for the Danuta Gleed Award and the ReLit Award), *Into the Early Hours* (winner of the Gerald Lampert Award; finalist for the Dorothy Livesay Award) and the novel *Stay* (*Books in Canada* First Novel Award finalist; *Globe & Mail* "Top 100 Books" selection; published in the UK by New Island Press).